The Divine Story of Ash

BASED ON A TRUE STORY

ASH MARINA

ISBN 979-8-88616-707-8 (paperback)
ISBN 979-8-88616-708-5 (digital)

Christian Faith Publishing
Meadville, PA
www.christianfaithpublishing.com

Printed in the United States of America

Ash Marina

Ash like my name

CONTENTS

CHAPTER 1

Divine Numbers

In the beginning…kidding…

One night, at the end of spring in 2019. I was watching a movie called, *Double Mommy.*

Alex came into the living room and sat down on the couch and said, "That's what I'm going to do to you. I'm going to put something in your drink and do that." In my head, I'm like, *Why would he need to do that?*

Alex started acting weird, so I started asking if he's cheating. He said, "You can't think like that. You're going to mess up the plan."

Another day, I asked Alex, "Are you cheating?"

He said, "I can't have you thinking like that. You're going to mess up the plan." I never thought of questioning it. I should have, but I just heard him, and I stayed quiet.

Alex left the room. Then Alex came back in and asked, "If there was a guy right here, would you have sex with him?"

I said, "I won't do it."

Alex said, "It's going to hurt but…"

Rethinking it, I should have questioned it. Weird of him to say something like that. Alex is too jealous. Then he asked, "Is there anything you have not told me? You can tell me, and I won't get mad."

I told him, "Just girl stuff with my best friend." Alex still got mad. I never heard the end of it. He was upset over me and my friend's girl talk. He is always bringing it up, as if I can't have a girl talk. Why is he arguing with me? I kept all of my side comments to myself, and I wondered about what Alex had said about the planning and that "it's going to hurt but…"

I started to see the numbers 21, 23, and 22. I started to see it on PinMe, clocks, license plates, and my job. Also, numbers like 123, but I only look at the last two numbers—121, 122, 123. I'll just care for the 21 and 23. Seeing 21 made me feel safe, 23 made me feel comfortable, and 22 made me feel scared. I was afraid every day, and seeing numbers 22, 21, and 23 alerted me. The color green was part of it too. I would notice green. My thoughts had become like a dream, making stories the same way as a person that were to have a dream, and they believed everything in the dream. For example, like a house, and you see a purse on the table, and in your dream, you know it's your house. The purse on the table, you know that your mom bought it for you as a birthday gift. When you wake up, you have never seen that house before, and you have never seen that style purse before, but it was real to you in the dream. You think everything in your dream is real, but you wake up and you realize none of the dream is true. It was my best example I could give on how I was thinking at the time. I would be awake at home or at work, working, my thoughts and thinking we're making stories, as a dream would. But I do not notice, just like you wouldn't notice in your dream. The number 4 was brought up to my attention too; 4, 21, 23, safe, fan of Ash, or the right place to be. Everyone that I saw who had green was on my side.

What alerted me was when I was sleeping. The second I woke up, Alex called me. He asked, "How did you sleep?" Then Alex said, "Be quiet, Marc!" on the phone. I didn't hear what Mark had said, but I had a weird feeling. I think Mark made a comment to what Alex had asked, "How did you sleep?"

One day, Alex was telling me that he wanted to jail break into the Zenobia stick. We went to his cousin Marc's house. I waited in the car.

My mind created a story that night at work. I work nights. I was texting Alex, and he was texting me differently, so I didn't think it was him.

My mind created a story. I thought Alex gave two of his male cousins, Jason and Kenneth, his HangBy account so they could take turns texting me. In real life, every time Alex would text me, I would think it's one of his cousins texting me instead. I wondered why his cousins were texting me instead of him. But I went with it and would text without saying anything.

Until one day, I had enough, I wanted to know why Alex was having his cousins text me instead of him. Why is he letting his cousins control the relationship? I started responding to Alex's text messages with "Leave me alone" or "I don't text hackers" or "Stop texting me." I would be upset because I thought it was his cousins texting me.

I was thinking Alex was screenshotting our text message to his family because his family kept saying things from my text messages. I confronted Alex with this while texting him. Alex responded, "I want everyone to see that you're the devil." In my head, I was like, *I'm an angel*. Is he trying to make me look bad to his family? So that's when I started thinking he's doing things to make me look bad. He's making me look like I'm an irrational girlfriend.

I was also thinking they were able to get into my pictures because one day, Alex and I went to a graduation party. One of his cousin's girlfriends was talking to me about her butt. I thought she brought up that conversation because she and everyone were seeing my photos through their phone, and she noticed my butt progress photos.

Also, I had sent a text message to someone that said, "Let me know."

Then another one of his cousins was talking to Alex, and his cousin said to him, "When you go to exercise, let me know."

At the graduation party, I was just sitting, and his cousin's girlfriend spilled wine on me by accident. I went home to change.

Another day, I was texting Alex about how weird everything was. I feel like everyone sees what I text message. He replied, "What are you talking about?" Everyone felt weird to me.

One day, I was talking on the phone to another one of Alex's cousin's girlfriends. She was telling me about her car insurance, and she also made a comment saying, "Oh my word." Then right when I hung up the phone with her, Alex called me and mentioned car insurance. I didn't think anything of it. We hung up the phone. Alex then called me right back, and for no reason, said, "Oh my word." Alex has never said *oh my word* before. I started thinking she's either doing a three-way conversation with me and Alex, or she called Alex and told him to say, "Oh my word" to me. This happened all back-to-back, at the same moment.

One day, I started getting scared. I cried for the first time, and it was loud. Alex called me. I was crying loudly on the phone. He was upset that I was crying, so while I was crying, a feeling came to me that Kenneth told Alex, "Tell her to calm down," and right when I felt that, Alex said, "Calm down." From then on, I started thinking Kenneth and Jason were listening to our phone conversations.

Alex would call me while he was working, and I would think his cousin was on the line listening. I would talk on the phone with Alex, and on the phone, while I'm talking to Alex, he would cough. It was like he was doing it intentionally. I'll say something, and he'll cough right after.

CHAPTER 2

Divine World

One day, I woke up from a nap. I had fallen asleep on the couch, Alex played soft ball every summer for years. But this year, Alex decided to make his own softball team. Every year, Alex's shirt number is always 22. He was the coach of the softball team.

Alex was in the living room making his team, his line up, and making the uniforms. Alex asked me what my favorite number was. I told him, "23," He said, "I think that's Kenneth's favorite number." Then, Alex asked me, "What color do you like?" I told him green. My favorite colors are aqua and pink, but I told him green because I like to wear olive green.

One night, I went on PinMe for the first time in a long time. I was scrolling down. I kept scrolling, just looking at all the photos. I started to get weird feelings. All of a sudden, the photos felt like they were talking to me, and just like a dream, I did not notice. It was as real to me as someone would feel in a dream. You will not notice it.

I was scrolling down PinMe, and a photo popped up by itself. I felt like it was Kenneth. I'm like, "Okay, you can control my phone and apps using your phone." I kept scrolling. A lot of the photos on PinMe were quotes about how you would feel in a broken relationship. I started relating that to me, feeling sad, lonely, and mistreated. Also, photos will pop up by itself about "love," and "falling in love." I thought it was Kenneth, so I said in my head, *That's a little too much.*

Every night at work, I would go on PinMe, and I enjoyed seeing photos of quotes that related to me and my feelings. Then I noticed the number 22 on the dates and time of the photos on PinMe. The number 22 was starting to scare me. The pictures were about happy relationships and being happy. I was afraid when I was seeing 22. Then I would read people's captions on my PinMe. I started thinking people were talking about me, calling me emotional and hurt. So I started thinking that the world knows about me. I wondered how.

Another night, I started to see a lot of the number 21 on PinMe—dates and times of 21. I liked seeing the number 21. It made me feel happy. So I started scrolling down and only read the quotes that had the dates or time that were 21.

One day, I started thinking that Kenneth was using quotes to make me happy.

The quotes would make me feel good. Every night, I was upset or afraid about Alex's family knowing my business. Then I started to get used to Alex's family knowing my business. I used PinMe to make me feel better. But I did start to isolate myself without knowing I was doing it.

Another night at work, I wanted to know why all this was happening and how come Alex wasn't telling me. Why did he have to keep it behind my back? In the morning when it was almost time to leave, the head CNA came in. She saw that something wasn't right with me. I had isolated myself. She noticed that, so she said to me, "You have to talk to someone about how you're feeling, like a therapist." I thought she knew about my PinMe and my feelings about being sad and hurt. So I was thinking, since she knew, then who else knew? How was everyone hacking my phone?

I started scrolling down PinMe for clues. I was trying to find out what was going on and what the world was saying about me using PinMe. I'm relating everything to me and thinking, *How do people know what is happening in my relationship?* I have a strong feeling that PinMe is talking to me.

One night at work, I was sitting. I looked at my phone, and a video popped up by itself on my phone. It was the news talking about the 4th of July. I questioned to myself, *What is Kenneth trying to tell me?* I just thought he was telling me that the number 4 was one of my numbers. It wasn't 4th of July yet. This was the beginning of June 2019.

One day, I had told Marissa that I wanted to leave my hairstylist. Marissa recommended a salon because she goes there. I then made an appointment there. On the day, I went into the salon. I was sitting down on her chair. My hairstylist was making my hair dye. I have ash-blonde hair; ash, like my name. I started to feel scared, so I looked all around, moving my eyes in every direction, trying to find the number 21 somewhere so that I could feel safe. I looked next to me, at another hairstylist. She had a hairspray-looking bottle that was factory made to have the number 22 printed largely on the bottle. I was so afraid to see the number 22. I started to think that Alex had a link to the salon, like if he owned it. My thoughts were like dreams. I took out my phone, went on my notes, and wrote, *Am I safe here?* thinking Kenneth will see it from his phone. Right when I finished texting that, the lady put something in front of the bottle that had 22. It blocked the 22 from me, so I wouldn't see it anymore. Then my hairstylist came walking toward me while looking at her phone, and she said, "Wow." I thought she had read what I wrote in my notes. Then I looked up to the mirror and saw a postcard-looking paper that said 4th of July on it. I felt relieved to see the number 4, and that made me calm down. So I thought, *Oh, she's on my side.* Then my hairstylist started putting bleach in my hair. She noticed my opal earring; she said it was nice. I thought, *People are able to see what I text on my phone by being on their phone.* Just how everything happened in that moment made me think like that.

One day, I was getting ready to go with Alex to a BBQ. When I was done getting ready, I walked into the living room. Alex was waiting on the couch, on his phone. I was thinking he was texting his cousins, telling them, "She's going dressed in her mood." I was thinking he texted them that because in real life, I wanted to dress in my mood, which was gray. I was going in the color of my mood.

When we got there, I noticed there was a group of Alex's family wearing gray. I felt so uncomfortable, thinking they were making fun of me. I was starting to feel bullied. His cousin said to me, "Ash, you're getting old." I thought he only said that because he saw the pictures of me, zoomed up in my face. I take pictures close up to keep track of my aging. I just sat down next to them with my head down and while playing with my hair. I was sitting, and Alex's female cousin spilled soda on me. Just an accident, it dried up fast. Alex later told me to go over to the fire, so I got up and went by the fire, and Alex's cousin's girlfriend said, "Oh, man." I always say, "Oh, man." I thought, *Is she watching me too?* In my head, I'm like, *I'm the only one who says that. Did she say that on purpose so I can know that there is something going on?*

One morning, I had woken up with blood. When I got out of bed, I went to the toilet, and there was blood in my vagina. I wiped and there was blood on the toilet paper. It didn't look period related; it was not old blood. It was fresh blood. I also wasn't near my period, and I didn't have sex even before I had my last period. I was very surprised and thought it was weird.

I can't remember the day I woke up with blood, either weeks or days, before or after, the day of the BBQ. I tried to remember what day I woke up with blood.

Like a week later, we went to New York for a softball game. It was Alex, me, and Jason. When Jason came in the car, he was like, "It was funny what happened with the colors." I thought he meant the day of the BBQ. Then we went to get coffee. While we were driving, I sipped my coffee. Alex coughed then Jason coughed right after. I started to think that Alex put something in my drink. I had left my coffee in the car when I went inside the gas station. They literally coughed as I was sipping my coffee. While we were driving, Jason said, "My favorite numbers are one and…" I couldn't remember the other number. I think he said twenty-five. I do not remember. It was weird how he mentioned favorite numbers at the time I started being alerted by numbers. Then while we were leaving New York, we were looking outside, and Jason said, "Looks like someone can get raped here." I was thinking, *Why is rape in your head?*

One night at work, I was scrolling down on PinMe, and a picture popped up by itself. It was a picture of a riddle. Since it was clicked on its own, I thought Kenneth wanted me to guess the riddle. The riddle was: I am used in most sports, have four holes, come in many different colors, and there is a state that shares my name.

So I thought about it. I guessed a jersey for the answer. I pictured a jersey with the number 23. The state that shares my name, I guessed Kentucky, Ken. So I texted Alex saying it was Kenneth. Then the lights at my job where I was standing blinked on and off. Remember, my thoughts were like dreams. If something were to happen in real life, my mind would create a story just as a dream would. My thoughts were based on real life events. After the lights blinked on and off, I thought that Kenneth was able to control the lights through his phone too. Alex just replied, "I don't want to deal with this now."

My mind would create stories based on my everyday life. I was crying almost every day because I thought quotes, Chirp, and Instycam captions from PinMe were telling me things that were happening. This was a way for people to be able to let me know things without talking to me because nothing isn't supposed to be said out loud to me directly.

At night at work, I was scrolling down PinMe. I started seeing the Letter M, and I started reading captions that said Issa. It was about relationships. Scrolling down, I saw more M's. I thought my cousin Marissa was putting these photos on my PinMe. Her way of telling me she is in a relationship with Alex.

I would scroll down on PinMe, and my phone on its own would click on a photo, usually quotes. I would see the time. If the time had 21 or 23, it was for me to see from other people. I would read them, and in my mind, I thought, People really know about my relationship with Alex. But mostly it was my cousin Marissa posting. She was bragging about her relationship with Alex.

I would keep scrolling down on PinMe and see the letter M, like M decoration and a lot of PinMe quotes and captions that said Issa. I thought it was Marissa calling herself Issa. Marissa's posts were the ones that said Issa and had captions about relationships. So I would scroll down PinMe thinking that Marissa is trying to have a little competition with me by using the posts that say Issa, who I thought was my cousin Marissa posting about her feelings and her relationship with Alex.

When I scrolled down, a lot of the quotes, Chirp, and Instycam captions were popping up on their own. I thought it was Alex's cousin Kenneth. In my mind, it was Kenneth on my side, helping me put out quotes about my feelings for people to view. So in my mind, Kenneth and Marissa were competing, but Kenneth was pretending to be me. Kenneth was the one posting my feelings.

Marissa posted things about her using Issa quotes and pictures of couples together. It was her way of telling the world how their relationship was.

Marissa would brag about herself and her feelings with Alex. Kenneth would post my feelings of being hurt by their relationship.

My mind created that Kenneth made a Phizbook for me. Kenneth was in charge of that account. He would post quotes pretending to be me because I wasn't on social media. The world will post on my Phizbook or post on their Chirp about Marissa's relationship with Alex or about my relationship with Alex, so you're either a fan of Marissa or fan of Ash. I didn't have any information about this. In my mind, Alex wanted to keep this from me. Alex had posted things like calling Marissa M. "My everything," Alex would call her.

Kenneth also posted people's posts on my PinMe what he would see on social media. So I could see it from my PinMe what people were posting about my relationship with Alex and what Marissa and Alex were posting too. I could see it on my PinMe.

Kenneth put quotes about my feelings on my Phizbook, which he made for me.

I then felt like Kenneth wanted me to look for pictures that relate to me and save the pictures to my PinMe so people would know what my feelings were.

In my mind, Marissa and Kenneth were also using my PinMe to fight each other. Marissa put her quotes and pictures, and Kenneth put his quotes and pictures; but Kenneth used my feelings.

I was scrolling down PinMe. Marissa had one side, and Kenneth had the other side. I kept scrolling down, looking at both sides, and they were fighting with the pictures. Marissa posted a girl in a wedding dress. Kenneth posted a couple having fun at an amusement park. Not every picture was from them; only some. Marissa posted a picture of a couple smiling together. It's supposed to be Marissa and Alex together. Then Kenneth posted a picture of a couple on the beach, hugging. It's supposed to be me and Kenneth. Marissa posted her skill; she does art, so Marissa posted an art painting on my PinMe then Kenneth posted what I did, which were squats. So Kenneth posted a picture of a girl doing squats.

I was scrolling down reading things that said Issa on it. I would save the ones that were popping up by itself, who I thought was Kenneth clicking it for me through his phone. I had pictures pop up by itself with the words NASA, and I would save it because it was a pop-up picture that was clicked on its own. I wondered what NASA meant, but I was like, "Okay, IDK. What does this mean?" I saved it anyway. When I save photos, it's for the people to view. Marissa posted more wedding dresses. So Kenneth posted a better wedding dress. It was fighting each other back and forth; but not every picture, just some, while I was scrolling down.

My mind was creating a story. I saw a picture that said, "He left his hoodie." I thought it meant Marissa was obsessing over Alex's hoodie. I was seeing a lot of scrunchies on my PinMe. My mind was taking it as Marissa was bragging about hoodies and scrunchies.

One morning, when I came home from work, I parked next to a car. When I got out of my car, I noticed a scrunchie in the car wrapped around the gear stick. I thought, *No one wears scrunchies. Is she hinting at me that she's the girl, the girl putting those scrunchies all over my PinMe and putting a scrunchy in her car because she knew I would see it? So I would know it's her, the one that is with Alex? I thought it was the neighbor.*

Later that night, I argued with Alex accusing him of talking with the neighbor, and the neighbor started banging on the wall. So I went back to PinMe. A video popped up on my phone, but it wasn't from PinMe. It was a video of a dog jumping between the doorway, but the dog was having trouble getting through, and the girls were laughing in the video. So I thought it was her way of making fun of me because I was a confused person trying to figure things out.

CHAPTER 3

Available

One night, it was my time off from work. I was crying on the bathroom floor. Alex came in and threw credit cards in front of me. So I got really scared. I got dressed really fast, and I ran outside. It was dark outside. Alex came outside. He jumped on the trunk of his pickup truck. It had a cover on the trunk. He sat down hard on the trunk as if he was cool. People were outside passing by, and I thought they were recording, and I thought he knew that they were recording because he was all tough on the top of his trunk, sitting. Alex then threw credit cards on the floor, same way as you would when you throw money. Then a lot of cars that were passing by looked like their headlights were flashing. I ran to the pile of cards and looked at what he threw closely. I got so scared, and I ran off screaming, "Somebody help me!" at the top of my lungs. I ran in the back of a building and hid in a bush. I was hiding from the streetlights because I thought it had cameras in them following me, so I moved in as close as I could inside the bush. I started thinking my belly ring had a tracker, so I took it off and walked to the stairs of the back of the building and placed it there, and I ran back to the bush hiding. I was thinking people were tracking me, and that they had to bully me. I was scared of people, and I didn't want to trust anyone. Even my mom, I thought she was on Alex's side. I stayed in the bush for a long time. Then, I was hearing a lot of cars passing by, making the sound *vroom*. My mind created a story that Kenneth had called Alex and said, "I'll take her home." So Kenneth called people to make a lot of cars go *vroom*. I was hearing a lot of *vroom* sounds. When I walked toward home, I saw two people at the stairs, where my belly ring was. I ran back fast and hid in the bush. Then I got out to check if they left. I was thinking those people were with Alex, and they tracked my belly ring, but they did not find me there. The two people were gone. I ran toward my belly ring. I took it, then I ran toward my apartment. But I got scared, so I put my belly ring on the ground, on the grass.

I walked to my apartment with cars going *vroom*. I was thinking they were making the *vroom* sound to bring me back home. I passed a window of the first floor of my apartment building, and coming from that window, there was a *vroom* sound. I thought those people were with Kenneth, and they were helping with bringing me back home. When I got home, Alex said, "What made you come back?" I said, "The cars." He didn't say anything. In my mind, Alex knew the cars were intended to bring me back home. My mind created a story. I looked on the table, and there was a bent Auto Ribbon card. I was thinking Kenneth was linked to Auto Ribbon, and bending the card and putting it on the table was Alex's way of letting go of Kenneth's link, and Kenneth took me in. I was thinking that both Alex and Kenneth had companies that they were linked to. Alex and Jason were linked together, but Alex let go of Kenneth's link and Kenneth took me in.

That morning, Alex and I looked for my belly ring. Alex found it, and I put it away.

That night at work, I looked on PinMe, and I saw a caption that said, "She just wanted to get kidnapped." That is not what happened. I ran away scared.

I started noticing that Wrendy's would take a long time to come on the intercom to take my order. So I was waiting for someone to say something. My mind created a story; they were tracking me, and it showed that I was waiting. They knew it was me, and they didn't want to take my order, so I left for Mr. Golden's.

I went home that night, and I was arguing with Alex about what's going on, telling him that people are bullying me. He would respond by saying, "What are you talking about?" The door to the living room was open. A loud long beep from a car sounded, and Alex put on a face like, "They are outside." I automatically thought there were people outside recording. He went outside, and I followed him. A girl walked by and coughed. I was scared. I went inside. I was thinking that the group that Alex was in did things like cough, long beeps, and flash their headlights.

I went to Wrendy's the next night. When I turned into Wrendy's, a loud long horn beep of a car sounded. I drove around and left scared. I was thinking, *Wrendy's was not on my side.*

When I went to places like the stores, someone would say something out loud, or they would reenact one of my text messages or reenact something that they had seen from a video of me. One day, I heard a guy say, "What are you talking about?" Alex would yell that to me when we argued. That made me sure that people were watching me and reenacting things that they see me do.

I drove to work at night. I noticed people who were driving on the other lane would flash their headlights. I thought they had flashed their headlights to intentionally scare me. Right when I got scared, the radio said, "Need help? Call 911." Then I thought, *Are they mocking me because they know I'm afraid?*

One night, I was crying in the bathtub sitting down. I was saying, "I want to commit suicide. I'm so scared." I got dressed and tried to wrap a cord around me. Alex picked me up and put me into bed. He held me in bed and said, "You want to smoke weed?" In my head, I was like, *I want to commit suicide, and you want me to smoke weed?* I closed my eyes. I wanted to catch myself falling asleep because I could never remember falling asleep. I do not smoke, and Alex does not either.

My alarm went off for work. I work from 11:00 p.m. to 7:00 a.m. I woke up and picked up my phone, and a map popped up by itself—a map for the GPS. I thought Kenneth was giving me a sign that he is tracking me. This made me sure that I was really being tracked. So my mind made a story. My belly ring was Kenneth's tracker, my pearl earrings were Alex's tracker, and my opal earrings were Marissa's tracker because I remembered my hairstylist pointed out my opal earrings. I think she brought it up to my attention because she knew Marissa was tracking me from it. I took off all my jewelry, put it away, and went to work.

One morning, I was in the bathtub crying. Alex was sitting on the toilet drinking a can of beer. We were having a serious conversation while I was crying. I was telling him, "My mind isn't thinking the same! I can feel a mental illness happening! I want to run away! I want to kill myself! You have to take me seriously!"

Alex was like, "Everyone is going to hate me for getting you in this." My eyes turned wide, I thought, *Who's everyone? My family knows too?* I wanted to know what was happening to me. What was I in? Shouldn't I sign a contract first? It's illegal to get me in something without telling me first. I was thinking maybe my parents were able to sign my consent. I felt something was wrong with my mind. I felt a mental illness happening.

In my mind, I was like, *Who's everyone?* But in real life, Alex had said there was a plan, like a month ago, and now he said, "Everyone is going to hate me for getting you in this." So my mind kept making up these stories, but I was unaware that my mind was making up stories just like you wouldn't notice anything strange in your dream. While having the conversation, Alex sat down with his legs spread out on the floor. Alex rubbed his ear. Alex kept knocking his beer. He would knock it over then clean it. This conversation went on for hours. During the time, Alex kept peeing, knocking his beer, then cleaning it. My mind started creating a story from watching Alex repeat a rotation. I was thinking he would pee when he was wrong, and he would drink when I was right. But I couldn't tell what knocking it over and cleaning it meant. He did this rotation in the whole conversation. Alex kept playing with his belt, taking it off, and putting it back on, repeating. If I tried to explain to him what I was noticing and that I know he was behind it, he would say, "What are you talking about?"

He then went into the living room and started playing his PlayStation.

My mind created a story. Everything that was bought from the start of his relationship with Marissa was bought by her. I got out of the bathtub, and while being naked, I started throwing things away that were recently bought. The things that were hanging on the wall, I threw them in the trash. A rope necklace from his softball team, I thought Marissa bought that for Alex and had put a tracker on it, so she could track Alex. Alex was aware that Marissa put a tracker on the rope necklace to track him. I tried to throw that away, but he didn't let me. His belt that he was playing with, I rolled it up and hid it in my boot. I thought Marissa had a tracker on that too. My opal earrings that I thought Marissa had on me to track me, I threw that in the trash. Alex was standing seeing me throw everything in the trash, naked, then he said, "Well done." I was thinking that he noticed that I was throwing away only her things. After throwing everything away, I closed the trash with my butt. I sat down hard on it to make it close shut. Alex looked at me. Alex then went to his truck, grabbed a paper of his softball line up team, and held it up to my face. A thought came into my mind that the paper was a contract, and if I ripped it, it would take Kenneth out of the softball team. I knew Kenneth was the one helping me, so a feeling came to me to rip it. So I snatched it from him, I crumbled it, and I threw it on the floor. Alex got mad and said, "I needed that for someone." He called someone and told him what happened. In my mind, Alex knew what it meant when I crumbled it. I was naked doing all of this. My mind told me I had to walk around the building naked. So I threw on my jogger pants and a spaghetti string shirt with no panties and no bra on. I put on my sneakers with no socks on and put on my Nike hat.

It was the summer of 2019, the end of June. I left outside and walked around the building naked, under my clothes. My mind told me to go get food. I went inside and got my keys and went to Tortilla Dip. My mind told me I couldn't eat with Alex because that would be closing off my relationship to someone else on my end and just have the relationship between me, Alex, and Marissa. My mind told me that I had to eat alone, not together, and that would complete it—me being available to someone else while being in a relationship with Alex. It completed it; it maked it okay. Alex had to clean the mess in the apartment on his own. When I got to Tortilla Dip, on the intercom, they sounded sarcastic to me. I was thinking that they knew it was me and tried to bully me.

I went back home but walked to our apartment's swimming pool instead. I sat down at the picnic table and ate. My mind said I had to eat, and I would be making it okay for me to be with someone else inside of our relationship.

My mind created a story. Throw away all the things Marissa had bought, walk around the building naked, and eat after, but alone. Alex had to clean the mess, not me. I couldn't clean it. In my mind, a feeling came over me that Alex was aware of what I was doing and what my intentions were—walking around the building naked and eating alone after so that it would be okay for me to open the relationship and so that I could bring another person in. (I didn't know a sticker from a new shirt had accidentally stuck on my spaghetti string shirt that I was wearing.) Alex found me outside. Alex yelled out, "You're outside without a bra!" Then Alex went close to me, ripped the sticker off my shirt, and threw it on the floor then he walked away. Ripping the sticker off and throwing it on the floor made the people that were watching and I know that he was giving me away to someone else, and that was making it official to let me go and invite someone else into our relationship. Before Alex had walked away, the guys whistled. Alex calmed down, came back outside, and sat down next to me. There were people in the pool. I thought they were listening to us and recording me and Alex. A guy was playing with his son behind us with the water hose. The guy yelled out, "The hose!" I was thinking that he was referring to me and had said it for me to hear. My mind said that I was making myself available. We talked nicely to each other and made up for the argument we had inside the apartment. We then went inside. I put back on my belly ring. I sat on the toilet to pee. Alex opened the door and put a pill in my hand. I looked at it, scared. I was still sitting on the toilet. I asked, "What is this for?"

Alex said, "You said you had a headache." I spent fifteen minutes on the toilet trying to remember if I even had a headache. Then I started thinking, *Did I even mention that I had a headache?* I couldn't remember; I started feeling confused. I looked on my phone to see what the pill was. *Okay, and it was for headaches.*

He never cleaned the apartment. I was hiding out all over the apartment where I didn't think cameras were placed. I looked at the news on my phone and read, "Tornado Hits." I thought it was a girl making fun of me about the messy apartment like a tornado hit.

The next day, I woke up from sleep. I read, "Earthquake." I left my room, and when I went to the kitchen, a cabinet door was open, and right in front, there was a big oatmeal showing from the cabinet, "Quaker Oats." I thought Alex opened the cabinet to show me the Quaker Oats so I can see it when I wake up to let me know that people are calling me *earthquake* because that is how I was acting. I would cry and scream. People see everything from the cameras.

I went on PinMe, and a picture of a lamp popped up. I was like, "Okay, I don't know what this means, but I'll save it anyway." Another day, I went on PinMe, and again, another lamp picture was clicked by itself. I saved it. Then I thought Kenneth was telling me that Alex put cameras in the lamps. The lamps on PinMe looked like an office lamp for a desk.

One afternoon, I had finished taking a shower. I could hear the TV from the living room. It was showing the first Spider-Man movie. From the bathtub, I reached for my towel that was hanging behind the bathroom door. As I reached, my towel fell on the floor. The second it fell, I heard from the TV in the living room J. Jonah Jameson's voice saying, "Throw in the towel." That scene was a man who found Spider-Man's suit in the trash that he must have given up. I thought, *What does that mean?*

The moment was like I reached for my towel; instead, it fell on the floor; then a second after, the voice said, "Throw in the towel."

I started becoming alert as if my mind was stimulated. I would cry in the bathtub, and when Alex came in, I told him, "I want to know what is going on!" I started to get dressed like I was being watched. I would cry a lot. I thought that Alex put cameras in our apartment. I was thinking maybe, "jailbreak" and "Zenobia stick" meant to hack into everything, and there were cameras everywhere I went. I was living in fear. My brain felt so stimulated from everything. Alex had to do weird things so it could stimulate my brain to feel scared and confused so I wouldn't notice anything.

One morning, I saw a fork in the toilet. Alex had also thrown a bent card in the toilet. I thought, *What does throwing things in the toilet mean?*

One day, Alex kept taking off his hat then threw it on the floor then picked it back up. I was like, "What does that mean?" He would also play with his belt, or he would scratch the back of his head up and down. I would think Alex was signaling the people who were watching, like it meant something.

I would look at Alex with a stimulated mind as if Alex and everyone had to make me confused to stimulate my mind when he coughed at weird times in our conversation. There were times he threw credit cards at me and put a bent Auto Ribbon card on the table. These were some examples.

The last time I went to Alex's softball game, I was getting ready in the morning. While I was doing my hair, my mind told me I had to wear the colors gray and green. My mind was telling me that everyone knew what my colors were. After getting ready, I went to the park. At the park, I was walking through the grass. I looked behind me. I saw Alex's cousin's girlfriend behind me. She looked like she was recording me from her phone. I was looking around in fear. My mind was stimulated. I saw a girl wearing sweatpants, and her pants were riding up. I thought she was mocking me because my jogger pants always ride up. I sat down, and I looked at my PinMe. An Instycam caption popped up from Kenneth, saying, "Feeling like a princess." For me and everyone to see, like if I was being presented with cameras watching me. I saw a girl run across the grass. I thought she was mocking me when I was running the night, screaming, "Somebody help me!" There was a girl sitting in a group with a green hat. I thought she came in the same color that I was wearing, her way of trying to tell me and everyone that she was in a relationship with me and Alex and that she was the one talking to Alex. I was wearing an olive-green shirt; I thought she came in the same color as me on purpose. Another girl was sitting across from me on her phone. Her phone was flashing a light on my face. I thought she was doing it intentionally, trying to put the flashing light in my face. I had thought that was what they would do in the group—they flashed the lights. These were some examples. Then when I talked to Alex's mom, the girls sitting with the girl with the green hat all laughed. I started to think there was a mini microphone on me that was able to hear me talk. Alex then rubbed his ear. I asked Alex, "Can you stand next to me? I'm really scared. I'm scared for my life." I heard motorcycles behind me and a carriage full of cans going by. The motorcycles were going back and forth doing tricks and making loud *vroom* sounds. I started thinking they were there to save me, to make me feel safe and protected. *Vroom* meant safe. I started feeling calm, then music started playing. Every time I would feel scared, the music would stop; then I would try to calm down, the music started playing again. I started being scared again, and the music stopped; then I would try to calm down, the music started playing again. Same rotation over with the music turning on and off. When the game was over, I went into the car. I sat on water in the front seat. My whole butt was wet. I thought Alex did it on purpose. I thought Alex wanted to mock me for having things spilled on me those two times. Alex was going to take me to his uncle's house, but I didn't want to go because I thought Alex spilled water on my seat on purpose. How else would water get on the passenger seat? I thought he did it on purpose as a joke for other people who were watching to see. I told him no, I wanted to go home.

I changed, and we went to the movies. We watched Spider-Man. While we were sitting, Alex kept moving his arms around. Then people kept coughing. It kept going on. I was thinking he was signaling people, and they would cough after. I went to sleep during the movie so I could avoid paying attention to his arm movements and people coughing.

That night I went to work, I isolated myself badly. One of the CNA's passed through my hallway where I worked at. She passed by me and said, "I didn't think you were coming in after what happened." I couldn't say my response to her; my mind was too shocked, thinking she was talking about what happened at the park and movies. She was watching the live cameras of me, and she knew what everyone was trying to do—stimulate my mind. What else could she be talking about? I had isolated myself and stopped talking to everyone at work, but I didn't let my problems interfere with how I did my job. I always finished my whole assignment by the end of my shift. So I never thought she was talking about my work performance. That morning, when I went to clock out, there was a guy and a girl in front of me to clock in. They were laughing together, and the girl had a water bottle. While she was laughing, the water bottle splashed water on me. I thought she did it on purpose to mock what she saw when I had a wet butt from sitting on water. Then when I was going to leave, I saw another girl from the first shift pass by me. She was wearing a mismatched blue sock and pink sock. She was walking with her butt moving a lot. I was wearing mismatched blue and pink socks on the day of the park. So I thought she came into work, wore the same mismatched colored socks as me, and started walking like that so I could see her mocking me when she came into work in the morning. I was skinny with a big butt, and it moved a lot when I walked. I thought she was mocking the way I was walking with mismatched socks on.

I was thinking that Alex broke into my phone and was able to see what was in my phone by being on his phone. Marissa, Kenneth, and Jason were able to see my phone by being on their phone too. I was afraid, I was trying to figure out what he was planning.

Alex was driving, and I was in the passenger side. I was looking out the window. A man in a truck looked directly at me then scratched the back of his head up and down. I looked at him with a stimulated mind. He did it the same way Alex would scratch the back of his head—up and down. I thought the man in the truck saw Alex do it in the cameras.

When I woke up, I started thinking that the key to my car had a tracker, so I went to my mom's job to trade cars with her so I wouldn't get followed when I go somewhere. I asked my mom if we could trade cars. She said, "Okay." I left to the parking lot of Compassion Medical Hospital. A loud, long horn beep sounded where my mom's car was parked. I thought it was them; they knew where I was at. I gave back the keys to my mom and went home scared.

One day, I went into my room. I had found a tag on my dresser. It looked like it came from the butt of a teddy bear. The tag said Forever 21. I had never seen that before. I called Alex, and he said he didn't put it there. I did not know how a tag that said Forever 21 got there. It looked like it was placed there for me to see. My favorite word is *forever* being with the number 21. I thought it was placed for me to see.

CHAPTER 4

Divine Path

The next week, I came home from work, and a news report popped up on my phone by itself. It was about sex trafficking with a lawyer named Alex. It was Alex's first name, so I thought it meant something. Jeffrey Epstein was caught with sex trafficking, and two of his places were in New York and Florida. Alex had brought me to New York for a softball game, and after, he wanted to take me to Florida with him for another softball game. Since it popped up on my screen on its own, I thought it was Kenneth telling me that I was in sex slavery, and I thought that was why I woke up with blood.

I started thinking Alex was having guys have sex with me while I slept. My mind put two and two together. I was afraid for my life. I told Alex, "Don't come near me, or I'm calling the cops." He left home.

I called my mom and asked her if she could bring me to the hospital. In the hospital, I sat down in the ER of Compassion Medical Hospital, waiting. A lady who worked there saw me and said, "I have heard all about you." I was thinking that she heard about the videos of me. My mind was confused. (In real life, my mom works at Compassion Medical Hospital. My mom probably talked about me to her, but that was not what I thought at the time. I thought cameras.)

Everyone in the ER felt staged to me. It was like they were acting out a play right in front of me, reenacting some parts of what they saw on camera. I had noticed things around me. A lady snoring behind me, she sounded like Alex snoring. I thought she was trying to sound like Alex, what she heard from the cameras. I would hear Alex snoring on the couch, from my room, when I tried to go to sleep in my bed. Alex liked to sleep on the couch. I slept in my room. My mind was feeling stimulated listening to the snoring. My mind started to think that Alex would invite them in and go back to sleep on the couch, snoring. Afterwards, I heard a sound. It sounded like a bed rocking. I was thinking they put that sound so they could chart how I felt about it.

I heard a conversation between a security guard and a worker saying, "I didn't want to do it, but I did it for him." I thought they were reenacting a conversation from a video. The security guard kept writing things down. I thought he was charting down my reaction toward it, how it affected me. The security guard got up and started putting on his belt. I related it to Alex playing with his belt.

I saw a man cleaning up a water spill on the floor. I thought he was cleaning it so it could remind me of Alex cleaning up a spill, repeated cycle. I did not know what cleaning up a spill meant. Does spilling things mean something?

I heard a sound of cans hitting together in the ER, but I didn't know where the sound was coming from. I remembered I heard that same sound at the park—cans hitting together. These were some examples. Now that I think of it, the whole world felt staged.

I was looking all around feeling afraid and confused. I noticed that the area where my bed was had sections with the numbers 21 and 23 by me. The hospital knew what my numbers were. I had to be with numbers 21 and 23.

This is what boyfriends do to the girlfriends when they are in sex slavery. People who are in it will confuse the girlfriend so that she won't notice anything strange when she wakes up, won't notice rape, and the confusion will make her disoriented. But I was told, in a way, so I was scared for my life instead of being completely disoriented.

The hospital would reenact what they saw on camera to monitor my feelings when I saw all of the weird things in front of me all over again. The hospital did this to monitor and experiment on what was done to the sex slavery girls minds. The hospital knew about me and knew what my color and numbers were.

The hospital knew what was going on. I thought they saw me as one of the victims and was waiting for me to come in. The hospital did not want me to know what was going on. They wanted to keep it that way—being unaware that I was in sex slavery. None of the girls knew. The hospital kept this information from them; they were not allowed to tell them that they were in sex slavery. The hospital just waited on disoriented girls in sex slavery. The hospital did their job without ever telling them.

I thought the whole world or just Summersfield had to confuse me.

I was scared and traumatized from hearing the bed rocking. The ER looked staged, like a play. After waiting for hours, the doctor came in and said, "You are showing signs of high levels of anxiety." I stayed the night. (Real life, my brain was so stimulated. The hospital was not staged, but it felt staged.)

In the morning, I went into the ambulance on my way to Section 12. I went into the ambulance on a stretcher. My mind told me, "This is where you have to go for you to win this. If what we did made you have a mental illness, then you lose. You have to come out of it without a mental illness." When the lady was taking my blood pressure, on the intercom of the ambulance, a lady asked, "22 or 21?" I was hoping for 21. I was scared of 22. The lady responded back, "21." I was so relieved and happy I was going to 21. I thought Kenneth got his team to save me. I felt safe I was going to the right place.

I was thinking I won, and I was getting out of this. I had bruises all over my legs from throwing myself on the floor to cry. I was thinking my belly ring had a tracker and a speakerphone; that was how they kept track of me.

At section 12, a lady said to me, "Don't worry. We are the good guys." When the lady said, "Don't worry. We are the good guys," I thought she said it because they were not going to reenact what they had seen on cameras, like at Compassion Medical Hospital to monitor my reactions. Another lady asked if I had any jewelry on. I told her, "Just my belly ring." She said, "Okay," and she let me keep it on. She didn't tell me to give it to her. I thought, *Weird.* So I was thinking, *Kenneth and the good team had to track and hear me while I'm in Section 12. Section 12 knows and has to be okay with it.*

My mind told me that I couldn't take any pills because I wouldn't get the million dollars. I had to come out of it without a mental illness, so I refused any pills, even Tylenol. The lady asked me if I wanted to put my mom down for emergency contact. I was thinking that she was on Alex's side, and I didn't trust her. But I put her down anyway. Green was my color at the same time 21 and 23 started happening. If I see people wearing green, they were on my side. I would feel safe around people who were with me.

The next day, we had to go to a group session. I sat down at the table with other people around me, and I started feeling scared. I was looking all around the room to see anything that would make me know that I was in a safe place. My levels of being scared were high. Right when my levels were at the highest because I wasn't seeing any signs, two guys that were sitting in front of me turned to a plant that was behind them. One guy put his hand in the plant, and the other guy turned it around facing me, and it had a piece of tan tape written with a black Sharpie that had 21 written on it. My levels of fear went down, and I felt calm and safe once I saw 21 taped on the plant. (But now in real life, I think back, *Why did they both turn to the plant? And it happened to have 21 on it.*)

A lot of the patients were wearing green; even the workers would come to work wearing green scrubs. I felt protected and safe. I was where I was meant to be. They were on my side. I noticed at Section 12, my area of rooms where I was staying, had rooms that were room 21 and room 23. Seeing 21 taped on the plant, everyone who was wearing green, and being in an area with 21 and 23 like at Compassion Medical Hospital. All these just made things more real to me.

One afternoon, my dad came to visit me. He told me, "God is working with you right now." I do not go to church, but my dad and mother-in-law go to church.

When I was discharged, I didn't go back to work right away. When I wanted to go to the stores, my mind told me I couldn't go to Stalmart because that was Marissa's side, and I would get bullied. But Kenneth had made a team so that I was able to go places, which would make me feel safe. My mind said I could go to the store Great Lots in West Summersfield instead because my apartment was in West Summersfield. I had to go to stores in West Summersfield. If I were to go somewhere else, Marissa's side would try to make me confused.

I started going to places in West Summersfield so I could feel safe around people on my side. Places like Mr. Golden's and stores in West Summersfield. I would shop at Infinity 21 because in my mind, they were fans of Ash. The cars with bright white headlights were on my side. I would drive, and people somehow knew I was driving past them, and they showed their bright white headlights or *vroom* by me, to let me know I was around people on my side and that I was being protected. My mind created the story that Kenneth came up with a team that was good to make me feel safe when I go out to places. I would still have moments of crying, and I would run away hiding from the cameras. When I was walking around my apartment trying to hide, I started to hear *vroom* sounds, and my head told me, *That means it's time to go back home. Vroom* meant go home. I spent too much time being scared trying to hide from cameras and people tracking me. I would drive up and down Lakedale Road, speeding, trying to drive away from the cars that I thought were following me. I would go up and down Lakedale Road, speeding for hours. Then I would start to hear the *vroom* sounds from cars, and my head told me that it was time to go home. When I was just driving to a destination, a car went *vroom*. I would think that they noticed me driving, and they would *vroom* so I could feel protected while I went to my destination. The cars with the white light headlights were on my side. I had kicked Alex out of the apartment.

One night before work, I was laying down on my bed. My eyes were closed, and I was thinking. Then I said in my mind, *God forgive me for all of my sins.* Then with my eyes still being closed, a white light showed in my eyelids, a loud pop sound came into my ears, and it felt like the top of my head opened with white sparkles. I told my mom what happened the next morning. I started to trust my mom again.

Thinking back, I questioned myself, *Were there people really hacking my phone? Were there people really tracking me and following me?* I was healthy enough to go back to work; no more crying. I rethought. I remembered. Alex kept rubbing his ear. So my mind created a thought. Maybe Kenneth was in Alex's ear, like they had a small device that no one could see. Then I thought, what if Kenneth was in everyone's ear at the time who was a fan of Ash? Maybe Kenneth was talking to people through a tiny device in the ear.

My first night back to work, everything was normal. I was just sitting with my coffee, and I had a thought. If Kenneth was in everyone's ear, maybe he's in my ear too. Maybe not from the ear, but from the mind, and as soon as I thought *mind control*, a resident from the room in front of me woke up and said, "If only she could have thought that sooner." Then after she said that, she started rubbing her hands together, and by doing that, her bed started making a rocking noise, like the bed noise you make during sex. Then another resident rang her call bell at that moment. I got up to answer it. When I walked to her room, there was blood on her bed. I noticed that this was room 121. The resident was in the bathroom that was inside her room with her pants off; she was blind. I put two and two together, and that made me think that they were trying to tell me something. The bed rocking meant a guy was having sex with me while I was sleeping, and room 121 "21" was telling me that this was the reason why I was bleeding, and someone intentionally put a blind resident in the room 121 to let me know that I was blind, as in unaware of everything. I noticed that the hall that I have been working at for years had rooms 121 and 123. I have been working on this hall for years, and now I felt alarmed by it. I looked at the lady being blind, I helped her, and I thought, *Why do I have to be blind?*

I sat down and thought, *Did Kenneth put a thought in the resident's mind to say, "If only she could have thought of that sooner?"* So I tried to talk to Kenneth from my mind. I asked, *What does four mean? Does it mean four sex partners? I have only had sex with three guys.*

So I tried to listen to see if I could hear him. I kept asking, "Does the number 4 mean four sex partners?" Nothing, no voice.

When I left work at 7:00 a.m., I was driving home, and I was thinking a lot about the rocking noises that sounded like sex and me waking up with blood and room 121 having blood on her bed and the resident being blind. I was rethinking all of that. Then a voice came into my head saying, *This is what we do.* Then my vagina felt like an on switch turned on, and a tingling sensation went onto my vagina. The voice sounded like Jason. I went home. Then from the kitchen, I looked over to my bedroom, and I pictured myself sleeping. Then that tingling feeling came again onto my vagina. It felt like my vagina powered on of tingling sensations. So I was right; they were in my mind.

One night, I was giving care to a resident. She said, "Oh my word" out loud. I was alerted, and she felt staged. I thought she said it on purpose, and she was an actor. Later on that night, I gave care to another resident, and when I was finished giving care to her, I was fixing her blanket, and she said, "One day." That alerted me. One day is one of my favorite words. I thought someone put that in her head for her to say that. Was that for me to hear?

CHAPTER 5

Mind Control

I was at home. My son showed me a colored picture of a snake. He said, "Look, it's a snake." Then I thought of Adam and Eve and the snake. I was sitting on the couch, thinking about it. I thought people were listening to my thoughts through their minds right now.

In the morning, I went to my mom's house. I was in the kitchen. My mom came to me with the Bible and said, "Look, there were talking animals," and she read to me the part of Adam and Eve. In my mind, I was like, *She's only telling me this because she was listening to my thoughts about Adam and Eve last night.*

That night, I went to work. While I was driving, I was texting Alex saying, "You need to get your family out of my mind." When I went to send it, a supernatural feeling came into my heart. It felt like my heart was powered on, the power was so high, the feeling was like a strong wind in my heart. I felt like I was going to die. I slowed down and parked to the side of the road and said in my mind, *Okay, okay, okay, I won't tell anyone, I won't tell anyone.* Then they turned it off. The supernatural feeling turned off.

I was thinking that Kenneth or Jason would never do that to me; it was not them. When I got to work, there was a nurse on orientation. I heard her voice in my mind. My mind created a story. She was the boss of a company, and she came to work with me to watch me closely because I had found out about mind control. Her name was Linda. I was talking to her in my mind, asking her if she could let me go since I found out about it. I knew Kenneth and Jason were in my mind listening.

I went home that morning, took a shower, and laid in bed. I closed my eyes. I was laying on my back. I felt my body straight, but my soul felt like it was going in a circle, like a pencil moving in a circle on a dot—my body being the dot and the pencil being my soul. My body was still on the bed, my soul moving in a circle. I thought, *Yay! They're getting me out.* Then they paralyzed me. I couldn't move. I fell asleep like that. The next morning, I fell asleep the same way, thinking that the circle feeling was going to take me out of mind control.

I went to work, and I heard my cousins in my mind. My cousin Kate was telling me, "To get out you have to meditate, but Alex has to show you." My cousin Kate was telling me that Marissa and Alex were getting married. Alex has to put one of his cousins in my mind without me being aware of it. Marissa and Alex fell in love, they wanted to be together, but they couldn't be together because Marissa and I are cousins. Marissa found out about a company. They came over to our city, and they brought some of their people to follow and watch. Then they extended their conglomerate in our city to get more people. It was an open-relationship company. It's dark; not a lot of people knew about it. It was mostly for relationships that wanted to be with the wife's family member. To be able to do that, you had to get in touch with that company. So it would be okay to be together, you had to sign a contract, and the husband and the wife's family member had to go inside the wife's mind, and they were able to read her thoughts. The husband also had to get one of his family member, like a brother or cousin, and put him in the wife's mind too. So it's the husband, wife's family member, and the husband's family member in the wife's mind. Since Marissa and Alex were getting married, Kenneth had to marry me inside the mind control, the mind control being the marriage. Alex had put two of his cousins in my mind. The wife was unaware of this, and she's supposed to live every day without knowing for the rest of her life, and the husband's family member would have sex with the wife while she's sleeping. This would make it completely okay for the husband and wife's family member to be together. People who were in the company would see you and automatically know that you're in an open relationship, and the wife was unaware. Everyone knew each other. The people in the company also would do things to let them know they were in the company, like signaling their camera with arm movements, throwing credit cards, coughing, beeping the horn loud and long, and flashing their headlights. The company also gave people things to hack into everything that the wife is around. The husband and wife's family knew; everyone knew. They have a reality show channel that their family and people in the company could watch. It's an open relationship, and they could see your relationship on the live TV. They could look at their phone and see whose wife was around them; the wife was tracked and followed. You could not get out of this company. Anyone who knew signs a contract. You could stop being involved, but it's dark. You're in it for life.

If the wife finds out about mind control, she would get a million dollars for finding out. No wife has ever found out. I had found out, so the lady had to watch me. Instead of treating me like someone who knows, they saw me as a threat. A wife has never found out, so they didn't know how to deal with the situation. The wife never found out about their relationship because they were in the wife's mind, knowing her thoughts, feelings, and intentions.

It was only supposed to be Alex, Marissa, Jason, and Kenneth. But Marissa hated me. She paid extra to have our family in my mind too, once she found out that I knew about mind control. This was what my mind created, like how a dream would, but I was at work trying to work while this was going on in my mind.

I have heard my mom, aunt, and my cousin Kate's voice in my mind. They would just go on and on talking in my mind, and I was trying to work.

All I mostly said in my mind was, *Please. I found out; get me out of this.* I couldn't say anything out loud. When I was around my family, we acted normal around each other, but I was hearing them talking in my mind. Kenneth and Jason never said anything in my mind, but Kenneth and Jason just gave me a feeling that it wasn't fair to them. They had to hear my family's voices in my mind. Everyone else didn't have to deal with an annoying family in the wife's mind or deal with the wife begging, scared, and agitated every day. Everyone else's wife's mind is quiet. The husband's family member just listen to the wife's mind while the husband's family member live their daily life at the same time as listening to the wife's mind in her daily life. The husband's family member knew as soon as the wife fell asleep and woke up and opened her eyes.

One morning, when I was sleeping, I woke up to Kenneth's voice and image. He was telling me that Alex has me in sex slavery, and if Kenneth and Jason get out, Alex will put two guys inside my mind to get money, and they would have sex with me while I was sleeping. Then Kenneth started crying in my mind. Jason said, "We want to get out, but we don't want other guys to come in your mind. We don't know how they will be with you, and my family doesn't want anything to do with this anymore."

Kenneth said in my mind, *This is illegal what they are doing. We want to get out. I can't do this anymore.* I was laying down in bed, listening to my mind. I got up on my knees and yelled, "What? No!" Then I screamed loudly at the top of my lungs. Then I screamed again. Then a voice said, "We don't like that. We don't like all that screaming, and you are not even eating either. We don't like that you're losing weight. We need our girls to eat." Her name was Linda. I was on my knees on my bed, in tears, listening to my mind. She said, "No one has ever gotten out of mind control, but we don't like all that screaming. You're giving out too much attention."

Kenneth's voice said, "They killed Franky." That's my son's father. I was thinking he was doing an open relationship too with their company. Kenneth then said, "But you can't feel anything towards it."

Jason said, "You can't think about it." Kenneth and Jason were able to get out of mind control with me, but they can never get out of the company. They can track him and watch him; everyone watches each other. Kenneth and Jason also can track them too, just by their phone. Their app was hidden. The way they work their app on their phone was by their mind. The people in the company all have something in them, and that was how they could get into your mind to kill you.

Linda told me to go to the phone store and buy a new phone, get out of Alex's phone plan, and change my number; then she would get me out. I quickly got dressed and went to the phone store. I bought a new phone, put myself under my own line, and changed my number. I went to my car and waited for them to say anything else from my mind. Linda told me to go inside another store and scream. So I went into the store and screamed twice very loudly, as if I was in danger. Then a lady in the store said, "Oh my word." I was alerted, and she felt staged because she used the words "Oh my word." I went back to my car. A voice said I have to keep my mind clear. I was so panicked, and I wasn't allowed to think. I was so afraid; it was hard not to think. The voice told me, *Go to grandma's*, meaning Alex's grandma's house. I parked across the street from Alex's grandma's house, and I saw Alex parked in front of her house with Kenneth. My head told me that if I choose Alex, he would take the million dollars and leave with Marissa. If I choose Kenneth, he would let me keep the money, and he would take me out of sex slavery. So Alex saw me and walked over to my car. Alex saw my phone box and said, "You bought a new phone?" Linda already knew I wanted to get out, so Linda told me to say to Alex, "I want Kenneth." So I said out loud, "I want Kenneth." Alex was mad. He walked to his truck and grabbed a bat and walked toward me. I turned around and drove off. I went to my aunt's house, and his family called my mom and said not to come over anymore. I was thinking because they were scared that I said something out loud. I was not supposed to say anything about it out loud. They did not want anything to do with it anymore. I could get them killed.

At night, I went to work. My mind said, *Your phone is being tracked. You're still in it.* So I tried to get out on my own. I took my phone that I just bought and kept slamming my phone in between the door. I took my belly ring off and threw it in the trash. I bought a new phone the next day.

Marissa would bully me in my mind and make me feel insecure. I was afraid to think bad about her because I didn't know what they were able to do with my body, I was living in fear. In real life, I was taking care of my residents, but every second, I was feeling tormented by my cousin. One night at work, I gave a feeling that I was upset at my cousin, and right when I felt upset, my heart felt like it turned on with deep fear in my heart. I stopped what I was doing, left the room, and started speed walking in the hallway, saying in my mind, *Sorry, sorry, sorry.* Then it turned off.

One morning, summer of 2019, I picked up my son from my mom's house, then I drove to my apartment, I parked in the parking lot, and Marissa started bullying me, saying things and putting negative images in my mind to make me feel insecure. Then my mind accidentally talked back to her, and Marissa said, "Mark of the Beast." Then multiple scratches went through my back in many directions. Then I ran out of my car and ran in a circle. I could feel a supernatural net coming onto me. It felt like I had gotten captured. I ran back inside my car. I felt something turn on, coming on to me slowly all over my body. I put my head on the steering wheel, facing my door window. I held my hands on the sides of the steering wheel, and I was paralyzed. I closed my eyes. My heart felt supernatural. My mom yelled out, "No! She's not going to have a life."

Marissa said, "I'm going to sell you. Oh, looks like no one wants you because you found out." I pictured myself being locked in a room and guys putting me to sleep and having sex with me, trapped, never leaving. I felt like I was going to die. Then Marissa said, "Someone wants you for 10,000."

Kenneth said, "I'll buy her." My son was bored in the back seat, so he jumped into the front seat of my car. My son started pushing my arm, saying, "Mommy." It hurt so bad when he was pushing my arm, and I said, *"Mmm. Mmm."* It hurt to talk. It was summer, so the windows were up with the AC on. My son accidentally turned the heat on high. I was already feeling like I couldn't breathe, and the paralyzed feeling they put on me was already making me feel hot inside. Now, with the heat on, I was suffering even more. In my mind, I was like, *Please come get my son. Please come get him.* Kate yelled out in my mind, *Kenneth got into a car accident!*

Marissa said, "I'm going to break the remote." The guy already bought me for $10,000. Alex knew what Marissa had done, and he shot Marissa.

Kate yelled in my mind, *Alex shot Marissa!* I felt so happy. I felt like Alex actually does care about me. Then Kate yelled out, "Alex shot himself!" She then said, "Why would he do that? Alex could have saved her. He could have saved her."

I got scared, and I moved to break out of the paralysis. My heart felt like static from breaking out—a lot of static around my heart. I thought that by moving and breaking out of the paralysis, the pill that Alex had put inside my drink had broken the connection with the remote, and they could no longer paralyze me. I kept saying in my mind, *God saved my heart. God saved my heart.* I drove off fast, and I called 911. I said, "Track my phone! My cousin is trying to kill me!"

I went to Compassion Medical Hospital and parked. Then my mind told me to go to Sea-Colony Health Hospital instead, so I backed up into a car then drove fast to Sea-Colony Health Hospital. I went into the parking lot of Sea-Colony Health Hospital. My mind told me, *That guy is tracking your phone.* So I stopped the car, opened the door, stuck my head out, looked towards the back of my car, and threw my phone out the door behind my car. Then I drove all around the parking lot to leave. I had reached a gate arm. It didn't want to go up, so I thought the guy and his people were trying to keep me in, so I ran through the gate arm and broke it. I went to the ER side, and Kenneth's voice said, "Go inside and tell them you need to be put under protective services." I was frightened and scared for my life and scared for my son.

The nurse had given my son something like a TV dinner and juice. My mom came for my son, and I laid down on the bed. My heart felt burnt. Kenneth and Kate kept saying, "You're going to go to hell. They took your soul." I thought I was going to die any minute. I was so afraid of dying. Kate said in my mind, *Drink the juice. It has the cure in it.* I got up and drank the ice-cold juice. My heart felt burnt, and the icy cold apple juice going down cooled my burnt-feeling heart inside, so I felt like it was actually working, and that it was really curing me. (In real life, it's just an icy cold apple juice.)

The hospital put me back in section 12, but in another section 12, from Sea-Colony Health Hospital. While I was there, Linda would paralyze me. I couldn't move, and I had to either stare at the wall with a clear mind or close my eyes and stay awake. If I don't keep my mind clear, I'll have to stay paralyzed longer. I would be in pain from staying in the same position without turning. When they told me that I could get up, I had stayed in that same position for ten hours. When I was afraid, Kenneth's voice would come to my head, saying, "I'm here."

One night in section 12, I was trying to sleep. My head told me, *Keep your eyes closed but do not fall asleep.* They gave me a story in my mind. My eyes were closed, and I was awake, afraid to fall asleep. I could see a story in my eyes while being paralyzed.

I have my eyes closed, and I was in like a big bubble. Outside of the bubble was the company's own doctor. This doctor was doing these movements to the bubble; these movements that he did were supposed to put me to sleep using my breathing. When I reached the very second of me falling asleep, he would do a movement to the bubble and say, "A little too early." Then he kept doing things to the bubble, and he could pinpoint the next time I fell asleep by using my breathing. He said he knew how I fall asleep very well. When I was about to fall asleep, I realized fast and tried to stay awake because I was so afraid to fall asleep, and the doctor knew this. He said this made it tricky. The people in the company wanted to put the sleeping liquid in me. He said if he puts the sleep liquid in me, it was risky because if I do not fall asleep while it was in me, then it could kill me. I would be at risk of dying because I was too afraid of falling asleep. They wanted to risk it. He put in the liquid, and he didn't get me to fall asleep with the liquid. He did these movements with my breathing to try to get me to sleep, so he was playing with my breathing in real life. The doctor could tell when I was about to fall asleep, then he did something to the bubble, and I started to fall asleep. Then the doctor did something and said, "Not yet." He said not yet because if I fall asleep during that time, he already knew that I was going to wake up fast right after. So he played with my breathing, and the doctor made me swallow. I was too scared to sleep. The doctor had a hard time putting me to sleep. Now the doctor had to risk me not dying while having the liquid in me. From the bubble, I dropped to a bin with train tracks, going past things like levels. While I was passing these stages, my tongue was moving on its own to the back of my throat. Then my tongue slid to the front teeth, in real life. They did the swallowing for me.

One of the stages, I was laying in the bin with wheels. I was laying down on my back. I saw my first partner in front of me, then the bin moved to my second partner in front of me, then moved to my third partner in front of me, then the bin moved to my fourth partner, but I couldn't see him, so I imagined me having a tablet, holding it up. I imagined myself zooming it up on the tablet to make him look bigger so I could see him. Then my tongue slid to the front of my teeth. I then dropped down, falling in the bin. I remembered to move my tongue to the back of my throat. As soon as I was dropping down, I moved my tongue to the back of my throat, and I won the levels. Then they showed me what would have happened if I didn't remember to move my tongue back. I would have bitten off my tongue while falling. They showed me a chopped tongue falling down. Also, they showed me a pile of dead girls who died in their sleep from that level of falling. The girls didn't know when to move their tongue because they were asleep. I stood up all night, with my eyes closed. I was the only one to pass all the levels. I knew I was awake, but it felt like a dream, like a dream thought. I was paralyzed. In the morning, I moved by accident, and the paralyzed part of my leg broke off from being paralyzed, so I said in my mind, *I'm sorry, I'm sorry, put it back, put my leg back.* Linda wanted money for winning the levels. She was mad that I moved because I was supposed to be asleep, so she paralyzed me so I wouldn't move. Since I was aware of everything they were doing to me, Linda was trying to train me for the stages to pass the levels of the sleeping girls so she could get money; but I was supposed to stay paralyzed, and Linda got mad, so she did the Mark of the Beast scratches across my back. It was like invisible scratches, multiple scratches all at once. Then she threatened me that she took my soul.

My mind told me that they were a dark company; not many people know. The husband's family member was able to put the wife to sleep and keep her asleep so he could have sex with her. Alex put two of his cousins in my mind. The husband's side of the family knew and wife's side of the family knew. They were aware of this. They knew the husband's family member had sex with the wife while she slept. It made it okay for both families. Also, they could view their channel. Marissa paid extra and put my mom, aunt, and other cousin to make me miserable for finding out. It is a dark company; but in that company, there was a dark, dark, dark, part of it where only a little of the company knew about it. Marissa was part of the dark, dark, dark part. The company offered it to her after I found out. She basically sold my soul to them as soon as I found out about mind control. Marissa owned me. They did this to girls whose souls have been sold without them knowing by their boyfriends or husbands, like me; but I had found out about mind control, and now I was aware that my cousin sold my soul. The girls that have been sold without them knowing can be put into this mind game in their dreams. They played for money. The girls were asleep while the owners played these mind games with them in their sleep. Some girls end up dying. But I was awake, so I was able to surpass them in levels and move my tongue to the back at the time I needed to. I wondered how I had the knowledge of needing to move my tongue at the right time. Like the girls who died, I was still at risk of dying in my sleep because they put a sleeping liquid in me to keep me asleep. Since I was afraid to go to sleep, and I fought to stay awake, I could die from the sleeping liquid. I couldn't fall asleep even if I wanted to. I was too afraid of falling asleep. I was traumatized by sleep.

Another night, I was sleeping. I woke up, I rolled over on my back, and it was like my body was sinking inside a puddle of oil. I fell back to sleep.

Another night, I woke up to a big zap in my spine. Someone zapped me; I don't know who. Someone zapped me in my spine to wake me up because they were going to kill me while I was asleep. They gave me a feeling they wanted to kill me. By this time, I was extremely traumatized from sleep. I was afraid of sleeping and not ever waking up again. I kept asking in my mind, repeating, *Who zapped me in my spine?*

During lunch, my mind told me, *I can only drink cranberry juice.* I kept catching myself making four lines with my fork. I wanted to know what four meant. When I would start to feel alone or panic, Kenneth's voice would say, "I'm here."

I wasn't allowed to think about that mind game, dream thought. They would get mad, so I tried not to rethink it. I was able to fall asleep one night, and I had a dream. I was with Jesus in a lake, and he baptized me. I saw what Jesus looked like.

When I was discharged, Linda still was torturing me. I would lay awake all day trying to sleep but never could because I was afraid to fall asleep. I was afraid of dying.

Linda kept putting sinister feelings in my body while I tried to sleep.

Most times, I would feel like I was inside my body, like being inside a box but the box being my body. Jason and Kenneth knew I was suffering. While I was in bed, I felt like there was voodoo in me. Sometimes I felt like the inside of my skin was falling—skin on my arms, legs, and chest, all of my skin falling inside. That feeling was the scariest feeling.

When they do voodoo feelings on me, I would tell them, "God wants me. God wants me. You're going to get in trouble." I would have a lot of days screaming and crying. My mom came two times to my apartment to put holy oil on me.

I had a time frame to fall asleep fast. When I dozed off, a sinister wind feeling would wake me up instead. Instead of having a dozing off feeling, it would be a sinister wind feeling. Laying down in bed for ten hours, the doze off feeling would be replaced with a sinister wind feeling that kept me awake. I thought Linda was trying to kill me by keeping me awake because I had a time frame to fall asleep fast. It was hard to sleep while being scared. Voodoo feelings while I sleep.

I needed a work note, so I went to section 12. While I was using the front desk phone to ask them if they could let me go upstairs to get a work note from them, I thought in my head, *I hope Linda doesn't think I'm going to tell someone.* Right when I thought that, my heart felt like it turned on with deep fear. I quickly hung up their phone. I started speed walking outside and continued to speed walk outside saying, "Sorry, sorry, sorry." Then it stopped.

The husband's family member knew the wife's feelings and thoughts. The cousins were attached to my mind, body, and soul. If Kenneth and Jason wanted to be in the dark, dark, dark part of the company, they could have my soul attached to them when they are in hell; but when Kenneth and Jason found out about hell and how dark it can get, they wanted to get out of it. Husbands or the husband's family member can take the wife's soul without her knowing.

You can imagine what I went through, feel what I feel. I felt like I had to rely on Linda because I was clueless about the sinister feelings happening to my body and why it was happening. I was in fear. I felt like I was stolen without permission. Words can't express exactly what I really felt. I started to sleep in the living room because I was traumatized by my bed. I slept every day on the couch. A lot of employees from my job would just see me and start praying for me.

One day after work, I was crying in my car in the same position that I was in that morning in my car—my head on the steering wheel facing my window with my hands holding the side of the steering wheel. I was crying, and a CNA came to my car and prayed for me. Right after she left, another person came to my car and prayed for me. I was crying because it was like I was living in a double world. Linda tortured me in my mind, but we still acted like employees together. I did my job and my everyday life. I had to be normal because they would kill me in my sleep. I do not know how both of them knew I was in my car and what made them want to pray for me. How did they know? What made them want to come to my car? How did anyone know I needed praying? I didn't know what to think anymore, so I stopped thinking that my job knew my business.

One night at work, I was sitting on a chair. An idea came to me. I started to wonder if they were able to close my eyes; so in my mind, I told them, *Close my eyes.* My eyes closed, and they moved my eyeballs. Then I said, "Wait. Do it again. I think that was me." So I stared, and they closed my eyes. They kept it closed and moved my eyeballs again. They continued moving my eyeballs all around, I ended up feeling sick from it. So I ran into a resident's bathroom, and I threw up. Kenneth said in my head, "I had enough. I'm getting help."

Later at work, in my mind, he took his tablet to a lady in charge. They were able to get into my mind. The lady was able to see what I've been going through with Linda. She saw all the torment that Linda and Marissa put me through. I was thinking I was going to be saved and finally get out of it. I was so happy.

I went home, I took a shower, and I went to sleep on the couch. I woke up from my sleep, and a voice said, "Nooo!" Then a second after, my heart felt supernaturally beating fast, it felt like I was dying. I felt like they were killing me supernaturally. I started to breathe slowly to calm my heart down. Then the supernatural feeling on my heart stopped. The lady that Kenneth had gone to decided to kill me because I knew too much. Linda was supposed to kill me in my sleep once I found out, but she used me to make money instead. My head was told all of this. I was laying down in fear.

Then the story changed. Kenneth and Jason gained full control of my mind control, so now it was Kenneth, Jason, and Alex listening to my thoughts only. This mind control was connected to my mind, body, heart and soul.

Since Jason and Kenneth had full control over my mind control, I felt safe, and it has been a very long time since I felt safe and not scared for my life. I was comfortable enough to sleep on my bed.

So I got up and went to sleep on my bed. I laid down on my back. I got a feeling that someone was trying to put me to sleep. He closed my eyes. My eyeballs moved, and I was put to sleep. I thought it was Kenneth that put me to sleep. I usually take ten hours to fall asleep. That morning, I felt safe, and for the first time in a very long time, I fell asleep fast. Ever since that morning, I had no trouble falling asleep. I was no longer afraid to sleep. I had not been paralyzed since that morning. It was weird because once Linda left my mind that night, she also left my job in real life. I had found out about her leaving the night I went into work. This was the end of 2019—October of 2019.

In 2020, I had went on an angel's website that could tell me my future. Every night, I would go to work then home. I was mute. I didn't talk to people for a year. I knew Alex, Kenneth, and Jason were in my mind. I just lived every day knowing that they were listening to my thoughts. I stopped accusing Alex of putting his family and my family in my mind, but I also knew he and his cousins were listening to my thoughts.

Later in the year, I started to talk to people again, and I was starting to get my personality back. I was trying to find myself again. I wasn't the same person I was back in May 2019. I just want to be Ash again, feel myself again. My name is Ash.

Ash as in the grayish-white powder from burning wood in a fire.

Ash, like my name.

CHAPTER 6

Presented to God

In January 2021, I kept thinking of going to church. I was still trying to find myself. I would sleep fine, and all the sinister feelings stopped. I put that behind me.

In February 2021, at night, I was sleeping on the couch. I woke up and closed my eyes. In my eyelids, I'm in a bin on train tracks, a dream-thought, like the dream-thought game in 2019. I was in a bin, and it was Kenneth and Jason pulling me through the tracks. They were trying to save me. I fell back to sleep.

The next morning, I was sleeping on the couch. Again, I woke up, and in my eyelids, I'm in a bin on train tracks, and Kenneth and Jason are pulling me, trying to save me. It felt like I was in hell, and they were trying to bring my soul back from hell. I fell asleep.

The next morning, I was sleeping on the couch. This time, I was woken up by something. I felt a supernatural feeling of life. If life was a feeling, that is what it felt like. Something of a supernatural feeling came into me, and it felt like life. I was able to compare how I felt before and after, before getting the life feeling and after it came onto me. I felt dead before. How did I feel dead all this time and not notice? I was able to compare before and after. I can compare a dead feeling to a life feeling now. I fell back to sleep.

The next morning, again, I was woken by something. This time I felt a supernatural air come into my chest, like a supernatural breath, into me. I fell back to sleep. I was awoken with a supernatural breath, then I fell back to sleep.

The next morning, I was sleeping on my back on the couch. I woke up, and I'm looking up at the ceiling. My head told me to keep looking up, eyes looking back, all the way looking back. I felt God's presence. I'm facing the ceiling, trying to look all the way back, then I fall back to sleep. That night at work, I was talking to Alex on video. I turned my head to the left to look over, and I turned my face, back facing the camera, and on the little screen that shows my face, was still facing left. I thought that was creepy. I started thinking I had a demon in me, and I caught it still facing left. I quickly hung up with Alex. I went to a mirror. I stared at my face in the mirror, and I said in my mind, *Show me something.* So I stared in the mirror, and he moved my eyeballs to the left. I had healed from the trauma, so I was like, *Okay, do it again.* I stared closely at myself in the mirror, and again my eyeballs moved to the left. Then I thought, *God is going to get mad at me for playing with the devil,* so I stopped.

The next morning at work, it was almost time to go home. I was sitting. My head was telling me, I couldn't think of anything demon-related, just God. I don't need to know anything, just know it's God.

That same morning, I was sleeping on my back on the couch. I woke up, and I was facing up at the ceiling. My head told me to look up, eyes keep looking back, laying flat on my back, looking all the way back until I can't anymore. My head told me to stay like that. A couple of minutes passed, and for some reason, I wasn't able to control my thoughts. It was hard too. I tried to control my thoughts. I felt God's presence, so in my head, I'm like, *God!* I stayed, looking back, and I said in my head, *It's God!* It was still hard for me to control my thoughts. God made my hand move. My hand tapped up and down, and that controlled my thoughts. And I noticed that, I thought, *He's smart!* My hand was over my stomach, and God made my hand pat on my stomach. Then I started to feel weak and shaky from being in an uncomfortable position, my head looking all the way back until I couldn't anymore. Then I said in my head, *Is it okay if I get up to get something to eat? I feel really weak.* God gave me a feeling that it was okay to get up and get something to eat. I felt surprised, like, *He's nice.* I always felt like God was predominant, so I was surprised his feeling felt nice to let me get up to eat. I ate and I went back to sleep. I felt like they were trying to present me to God that whole time.

That night at work, I was sitting in my chair drinking coffee. A white light outlined my body all over. So I was drinking my coffee and looking at the white outline all around my thigh. It looked like a white aura all around me. My head said that I have to wait. So I was waiting and looking at the white aura outlined on my thigh. It was demons telling me to wait. The demons were making me feel like a princess. They told me I wasn't allowed to think anything demon related. A feeling came to me that I needed to stop thinking that Alex, Jason, and Kenneth were in my mind. I even said in my mind, *You guys are making me feel like a princess.* So I was drinking my coffee, waiting, and it's like thirty minutes of waiting. So I asked, "What am I waiting for?" They responded, "You are waiting for God." It was almost an hour. I stayed waiting, drinking my coffee, and looking at the white aura all around my thigh. Then I said, "God, forgive me for all my sins," then something white was thrown at me, and I felt God's presence, and ever since that night, God has been with me, living inside me.

CHAPTER 7

God's Way

The next morning, I came home from work. While I'm eating at the table, I heard a voice that said, "Wife, wife." I felt a little nervous. I stopped eating. Then I felt an intimate feeling. I felt confused because it felt like God. I went into the shower, and again I heard a voice that said, "Wife, wife." I didn't want to think, *What does that mean?*

After my shower, I laid down, and I closed my eyes, then an intimate feeling. And our connection felt like soul ties.

At work that night, I was listening to pop songs, somewhere sexual. I had a feeling that God was mad at me and ignoring me. He didn't like the music. So I got mad at him because he was mad at me. It was time for me to go home. I parked at my apartment's parking lot. I was still mad at him. God was trying to tell me that he is not mad. I was just thinking how mad I was. A song came into my head, "Help Me Find It" by Sidewalk Prophets. I ignored it and stayed mad at him, then he pushed my back. But it felt like he pushed my soul, and he said, "Get out!" I was surprised, like seriously, *Did you just push me? I'm a girl.* That was a little hard. The moment was like, *Boom,* "Get out!" I went to take a shower, then I rethought it. And I started crying because God was trying to calm me down, but I was too mad to notice. Then we made up.

Thinking back, the Divine used Kenneth's presence in place of God temporarily. Also, that morning, when the story changed, it was angels that changed the story around. It wasn't Kenneth who put me to sleep that morning. It was God who put me to sleep. I felt safe, and for the first time, I fell asleep fast. God was in control the whole time.

I would take a lot of hours to fall asleep, but in the hours of trying to fall asleep, I dozed off and woke up fast. I got scared when I felt myself falling asleep. When I was awakened by something in my deep sleep, I would fall back to sleep fast within seconds after being awakened.

Alex, Kenneth, and Jason were never in my mind. Alex never was in a relationship with Marissa. My family being in my mind was not real. My mind created the open relationship story, but demons intervened by using my family and Alex's family's voices.

Ever since that night, God has been with me. God gave me a supernatural feeling to let me know he's there. I could feel his presence, and he made me aware that the supernatural feeling was him. God felt like he was living inside of me. It felt like God made a home inside me.

One day, in May 2021, I was thinking of going to church. I told my dad that I wanted to go to church with him. The following Sunday, I went with my dad to church. When church was over, I met with the pastor. He asked me if I had visited any future-telling websites, and I told him yes, an angel website. He told me those are bad. He asked me questions. Then we did the Prayer of Salvation.

When I think and get out of focus, God makes my finger tap up and down. That gets me to focus. He does that to me a lot. If I think of something, he'll show me his reactions by putting a smile on my face, a sad face, putting my lips to go straight, or putting an unsure reaction with my lips. God puts facial expressions on my face with his response of how he feels so I can know what he thinks. God moves my lips to go side to side. It kind of feels like a rabbit moving their nose. That usually means a no. If God says no to me, to let me know for sure that it is a no, he'll make me wink and swallow. Like "No," then makes me wink and swallow at the same time. Let's say I break something of mine by accident. He'll put a sad face on me.

Let's say I go to the bathroom, and it smells. I think, *Ugh, it smells, and I have to shower.* Then God wrinkles up my nose for his response. Every second he's with me, living inside of me, I'll wonder, *How is he with me every second but still on the other side of the world too?* I would say a small joke like, "God is not helping you right now because he is too busy with Ash."

One morning, I had a dream that I was walking. A big black hole was in front of me, and I walked into the hole and fell. I was falling, and while I was falling, I got a feeling that I already knew that God was going to save me, and as soon as I felt that, a rope was thrown down to me, and I grabbed it, and I was getting lifted up. When I woke up, I remembered the dream, and a voice said, *That's how big your faith is,* because I was falling, and I already knew God was going to come get me.

Demons started to torment me. I would cry every day and every night at work. It was really bad. I would cry at work. My job said I couldn't go back to work until I got a doctor's note.

I was hearing my son's voice in my mind, *Mommy, Mommy.* I would hear a voice saying, *Your son, your son.* I was thinking that my son was fine. Those voices went on for almost a week.

Demons started to torment me, so I would sleep at my mom's house in Summersfield and wake up to pick up my son from the bus stop in front of my apartment in West Summersfield. The kids had just started going back to school after being homeschooled because of COVID. One day, mother instincts kicked in. I felt like something was going to happen to me. So I went to Stalmart and got a copy of my apartment keys and gave it to my son. When I went home, I showed my son how to open both doors to the apartment. I told him to keep the keys in his backpack, and I put his tracker in his backpack too. My mom and I are able to track him.

One day, demons were mad, and they kept saying, "Exorcist, exorcist." I went to sleep thinking a demon was going to possess me.

During my sleep, I woke up to a voice telling me, "You can't move. Don't move. You can't open your eyes. He has to do it." I can feel his eyes moving inside my eyelids. My body felt all sinister, supernatural inside. God kept holding my breath. He kept holding my breath over and over again. I was thinking God was trying to kill me because he kept holding my breath. I guess God was just saving me. I fell asleep. Then I woke up, and I moved by accident, and my leg felt like a knot. The sinister, supernatural feeling in my body made me feel that if I moved slightly, I would feel a knot at the part that moved. I accidentally opened my eyes, and it was all gray. I closed my eyes, and I thought, *This is real. A demon is trying to take control.* So I tried to hold my sinister, supernatural feeling body to stay still. Then God started holding my breath for a long time, and I fell asleep. I woke up to a supernatural air into my chest—a supernatural breath feeling—with my eyes still closed. I fell back to sleep. When I woke up again, I accidentally opened my eyes. Everything was still gray, so I closed my eyes, but I stopped feeling tired. So now, I was just with my eyes closed but wide awake, and I was feeling his eyes move in my eyelids. A voice kept speaking to the demon, telling him, "Open her eyes. Open her eyes," the voice kept repeating that. I was feeling like I was suffering. My body felt sinister inside, and I felt like I had to hold my body up and steady. I was feeling like I was suffering. That demon gave me a feeling that he felt bad, then he opened my eyes for me. God took him out. I told my mom to call the ambulance, and I ended up being hospitalized.

Another day, when I was hospitalized, my son needed to use the spare keys. Something was trying to warn me about my son. My son probably would have gotten kidnapped or dead. I had lost my job while being hospitalized. My son and I moved in with my mom temporarily.

God came to me, and he awakened me. He let me know for sure that he is with me every second. God gave me a supernatural presence to let me know for sure that he is with me, and God could take away that supernatural feeling if he wanted to, God said, "Would not." I wouldn't want him to take it away either. I love the feeling.

I asked myself how come God lets me feel these supernatural feelings, which made me aware that it's really him. I do not know why God makes it clear to me that he is inside me. He really feels like he made a home in me. I can feel God inside of me.

People cannot feel sinister feelings in the body because it is not humanlike, so feeling all of these sinister things happening to my body made me believe I was in danger. The demons didn't want me to say anything. They made sinister feelings to my body to go along with what my mind was creating. My mind created mind control, but demons used my family's voices, telling me they took my soul. I could think. The voices are all in my mind. It's just a little chemical imbalance, but nothing could explain the sinister feelings with my body. They made my heart feel like it had an on switch.

My story is what happened to me. I already "thought" everyone knew my business anyway. It's fine if everyone knows. I am a witness that the supernatural was here first; believe it. This is a supernatural world.

God is my everything, and Jesus is the King. I do not understand why Mary is being mentioned so highly this long. She just gave birth to Jesus; that's all. She was "just" a vessel. Bye, "woman." She is left at Jesus's resurrection as a normal woman with a regular burial on earth, just like everyone else. Jesus did not do anything special with Mary. She cannot hear any prayers. Mary is not at the throne with God and Jesus. After Jesus's resurrection, they moved forward. They do not consider Mary as the mother of Jesus. She is like a regular woman to them. Mary, living a "sinful" or "sinless" life, did not matter to God. He did not care if she sinned or not because he did not "plan" on having her continue after death, and that is not being "blessed." She is not "personally" special to God; that is why he picked her. The insulting part is, no sexual intercourse, no sexual contact, she was left with a virgin pregnancy. God was not sexually aroused. She did not need to be without sin. She had to be "at least" a virgin. "It's about a virgin birth!" The important part, "God wanted a virgin." "A virgin birth," and he "implanted Jesus" into her uterus without having a fertilized-egg process. Blessed without using her egg process? It is not mentioned in the Bible. You will not see her in heaven because after her death, she did not continue. Truth, there is no Mary in the afterlife. She was not reborn after her death, and she is not ever going to be reborn either. All I know is, she isn't anywhere special, and she is not special. Do not believe the internet if it's not mentioned in the Bible. "Woman," kind of harsh, right?

I would not be able to look at her in the face anyway, not with my mother instincts. It's a mistaken impression. What is it "NOT" about? And what "IS" it about? It is NOT about her being devoted. It is about her not having mother instincts.

Therefore, she had no mother instincts to stop it. She is not a real mother to them, and being a surrogate doesn't make you a biological mother or even a mother because she wasn't a mother before being a surrogate. It means she doesn't have "parental rights" to Jesus. For example, to understand better, in 2021, a surrogate has to "give up" the baby once the baby is born to the biological parents. The surrogate cannot claim to be the legal mother, and if she does try claiming the baby as her own, there will be a lawsuit against her! They do not consider Mary a mother because of no mother instincts. "Not special to God." That is why she was chosen, highly favored, preferred. Highly favored should be insulting. With no mother instincts, she can't keep her children safe. Mary made it easiest; she didn't know about safety.

My side comment, circle of women chosen from the bad-mom category.

Mother instincts are beautiful, special, and unique to God. God loves mothers. Not stronger, easier.

I have to think Jesus is a God and a man who was able to endure pain. "Pierced with a sword for being a woman without mother instincts." She is not in heaven. You will not see her there.

Mother instincts make a complete package in a woman, a "high-value woman."

She shouldn't have considered herself being a servant. "No, Mary, you used the wrong word." Being a "woman servant" is the feminine way; means Jesus would have not died on the cross or tortured. God's will? Yes, her trials were, like, for a man. "She has no mother instincts. That is the reason why God chose her." Highly favored to fulfill. I can see men doing wills like that.

An example to understand more, living in 2021, people are trying to honor a woman that would have had a social worker in her home, who at the time was trying hard to be perfectly poor around people because she got the "wrong idea about herself." "Pierced for being just a woman."

Mary should not have said, "From now on all generations will call me blessed." Where? That is too high, Mary. "False impression." Her words, "not God's words." And get out of her way. God never told her or angels that she would be blessed. Instead, she damned generations who followed that. It's a "get your own way" statement. You're making it about you. Mary changed and tried to be perfect and holy after she was told the news by the angel. The news made her want to persuade as holy because she got the wrong impression. There's a difference between Mary and a person having the Holy Spirit and changing their life around, a big difference.

God did not test her on anything. There is no what-ifs with her because if there was, then "she would not have been chosen." Was she being proud? Yes. "God gave her free will. It's not his fault if she was acting misleading." "Found favor with God," meaning, "be able" to bring his son into the world—nothing more.

Why the sorrows? "For the Mighty One has done great things for me." Nothing was mentioned "about" you. Having sorrows is not being blessed. The reason is, no mother's instincts; avoid mistaken impressions. You're the one being proud. Why aren't you fearing God? "Thinking" too highly for being "just" a vessel.

Jesus wants to be only beside his Father. When Jesus left her body, so did the glory. And holiness left along with him. With no mother instincts, she lost her chance to carry a "son," but there's no what-ifs, then she would not have been chosen. For that reason, the way God did the pregnancy, it was legal "only" on God's part. Surrogates cannot claim.

God needed Jesus to make him a "better Father" and to forgive all sins. God said everyone is treated equally.

But my story, not hers. Moving on, like they did. Too much Mary!

I wanted to erase it, but God said, "No!"

Jesus is beside God on his throne. God has been waiting for me. It's because I'm Ash.

Ash, like my name.

One day, I was sitting on the toilet. I held my breath so that God will make me breathe himself. I was sitting, holding my breath. I told him, "I'm going to keep holding my breath until you make me breathe." God started moving my lips side to side. I was like, "Make me breathe." So he moved my lips side to side—fast, then stops, then side to side, fast again, then stops, then moves my lips again, side to side, fast. It has a rabbit feel to it. So I was just sitting, holding my breath. It was quiet, and my lips were just moving side to side—fast, then stop, then side to side, fast.

I asked God in my head, *Do you use omens to tell you things?* God moved my lips side to side. That was a no. Get off that thought.

I asked myself, *Why did this happen to me? Did the demons see that God wanted me and decided to give me sinister feelings maybe so I can commit suicide?*

I felt stolen. It was always God. Demons intervened by telling me they took my soul.

I love how God came to me. I wonder if this could have waited until after I died? How I am now will be the same after death, as if I never died. I'll still be alive after death. I feel awake now. I was not seeking God, but I did think, God is in my heart. God came to me and awakened me. After death, you will still continue.

When I first started having conversations with God in my head, he started off making me wink or put a huge smile on my face. When he put a huge smile on my face, I thought, *No, too big. This smile is not cute.* Then when we had conversations around people, God would still make me wink or smile huge around them, and I thought, *No, people might see. They might think I'm doing it to them.*

In August 2021, I was hired for another 11:00 p.m. to 7:00 a.m. night position. At work, my side of the hallway where I work has room 221. The last two numbers were 21.

God and I would listen to music together all night. God gave me a supernatural presence; it lets me know that he was with me. I knew I was not happy without him. I would feel miserable and not motivated.

I really did live in a Divine World once God showed that he wanted me. I could imagine my old age being different from everyone else's on deathbed. When I die, I'll have God's supernatural presence in me. It will feel like he's actually with me in my last minutes of being alive. I can imagine before I die, he would be right with me, from life to death and afterlife. I love him to death and forever.

It is October 23, 2021. I plan on living every day with God in the future. God is living inside of me. He is involved in everything in my life. God puts his reactions on my face using facial expressions toward what I think or do. He always directs the bad thoughts away and gets me to focus by tapping my finger up and down. He gives a supernatural feeling that lets me feel what he feels. God is with me every second of the night and day. He makes it very clear to me. I can feel him inside me. I love it, badly.

I wish I knew God's plan. Not knowing overwhelms me. I put both my hands covering my face. I stay like that for a couple of seconds. I ask, "Why is this happening to me?" It gets overwhelming at times. I have so many questions. I do not think of ideas or anything because I do not know. I do not want to guess either, just have a clear mind.

I just know what is happening right now, which is God responding to me. Maybe I'll ask one day.

I'm awake at night, and I sleep in the daytime. Every night is a new beginning.

At night, God is awake.

Ash, like my name.

MY FAVORITE SONGS

"Help Me Find It"
Sidewalk Prophets

"Truth I'm Standing On"
Leanna Crawford

"Just Want You"
Sarah Reeves

"Fires"
Jordan St. Cyr

"Jump"
NONAH

Early in the day, November 23, 2021, during my sleep, Alex messaged me asking if I could take a picture of my car. He also asked if I could take a picture of the front of my car with the lights on. I read the message when I woke up. I couldn't help but to reminisce about the time I was noticing white headlights. It brought back feelings and memories. I didn't want to reply back "Weird. Why do you want me to take a picture with my headlights on in the daytime?" I moved past all of that. I didn't question him. I turned on my headlights and took a picture, with the sun still out.

I do not know why Alex wanted a picture of my car. He just responded back, "I wanted to see how it looks." Alex and I have broken up. Alex does not know my whole story.

November 23, 2021, at night, I was driving. I noticed how big and pretty the moon was—a waning gibbous. I was at a red light. Another car on the other lane was across from me waiting in front of the red light too. I noticed how pure white the headlights were. Right when I noticed the headlights, it turned on and off, completely off then on, then I saw an ambulance coming in the same lane of that car. A lot of cars were behind that car. The ambulance had his sirens on, the light turned green, and the ambulance drove right by me. The Divine World had stopped a long time ago. This moment reminded me of when I was in the ambulance, and the lady said 21 on the intercom. I turned into my street, and I could see how pretty the moon was.

I remember a couple of weeks ago, I woke up from my sleep. When I opened my eyes, a voice said, "I am going to blow up the moon." God knows how much I love the night and moon. I started wondering if he could make me a small moon to fly to and surprise me with it—a surprise gift. I know he hears me thinking about it.

It was night; I would be going to work soon. God was awake with me. I love tonight's moment with the moon and white lights, 21. "Lovely."

Ash, like my name.

December 3, 2021, I was on my laptop, reading and editing. I remembered an event that happened back in 2019. I was picturing what had happened. My hand was on my cheek, then the inside of my arm shook. God said, "You should have written that." In my head, I said, *Wait.* I felt lightheaded. I put my head down. I thought, *Hold on. That was a little strong.* Then I thought, *I'm going to add in this moment too.*

I adore these moments, badly.

All things good.

God signed, **O**

Put inside

God said I was put inside the body a little before
everything started happening.
My thoughts had become like a dream. I was alerted by the world.

I have memories of a different person.
In my memories, I don't recall being present.

"Later in the year, I started to talk to people again, and I was starting
to get my personality back. I was trying to find myself again. I
wasn't the same person I was back in May 2019. I just want to
be Ash again, feel myself again."

I can compare the difference, and I thought it was me. I have been
comparing since 2019.

"Kenneth posted what I did, which were squats. So Kenneth posted a
picture of a girl doing squats." Squats are from the memories of a
different person. I don't recall being present in those memories.

She had confidence; I'm more insecure, just girly.
One night at work in 2019, I compared. I thought, *I feel girly.*

She was sexual—I thought that was too much; I was listening to
     sexual music to compare.
Her personality was silly; I felt more mature.
She was depressed; I felt happy inside even with everything going on.
And it was easily compared, so noticeable, that I thought it was me.
          One night at work in 2019, I was sitting, and I
          compared. I thought, *I feel happy.*
I felt like I was just born as an adult—a virgin at life. Alerted by the
     world.
               Born a wife, puppet in my own life.

In 2022, I realized that the memories are not me; and thinking back, there
     was a change. I was more insecure. I don't feel like the way she did.

In December 2023, I kept getting a memory coming back to me and
     a voice saying, "Placed." Every time that memory pops up, a
     voice would say, "Placed."
After weeks, I put two and two together. Knowing my story, I con-
     firmed if that was what it meant; and we decided that I should
     write a short story, not "placed" but "put inside."
God said, "Made a wife."
Long ago.

          "Made a wife." Puppet in my own life.

January 2025, I won't be keeping memories or that I have a book. I
     can be taken out anytime.
God said too young to be a mom; no period—"You're immortal." Been
     same age for eternity. I'm a fairy. Locked in a room is where puppet
     came from.
God said took egg.

My thoughts and feelings are connected by the world.

God said I was put inside the body to save the boy.
God said worse than death. Something devastating.

God signed, **O**

Ash as in the grayish-white powder from burning wood in a fire.

Ash like my name

<u>*Mother Instinct*</u>

"You're able to safeguard your peace by keeping your promise, and having compassion with awareness."

"Trust yourself before you can have Trust in others."

Ash like my name

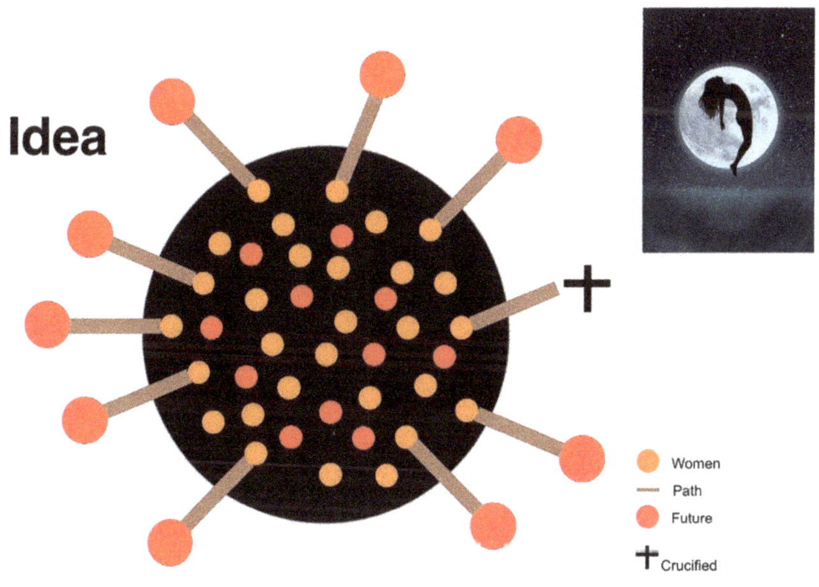
Idea
Women
Path
Future
Crucified

<u>**Love Language**</u>
The Narrator of My Story
Puppet in my own life.

Divine Path
1 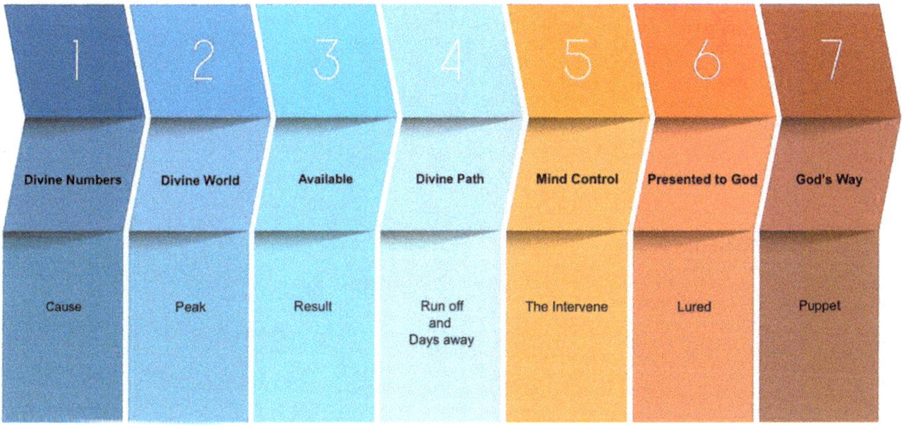
2
3
4
5
6
7
Divine Numbers
Divine World
Available
Divine Path
Mind Control
Presented to God
God's Way
Cause
Peak
Result
Run off
and
Days away
The Intervene
Lured
Puppet

My name is Ashleah Marina De Luna. I have a son; he's my world. I always thought of myself as having a heart of an angel. I have not been to church since I was seven years old. I never knew how to pray, but I would always think that God knows what is in my heart. He was always in my heart. I like to help my residents for a living. I love what I do, making sure my residents have the best of care. They would tell me that I'm a saint or was Godsent, but I just like to say, "I have a heart of an angel." It sounds really pretty. I always follow my heart, and I put my heart first in any situation I face. The Divine World continues. It's my thoughts and feelings. Sweet as can be. "I feel like an angel." (Goody two-shoes.) I was not seeking God. God came to me. He found me, and God put Himself in my life.

Now I live every day with God's supernatural presence in me. It feels like he's actually with me.

My name is Lia De Luna.

THE FRONT DOOR

I'm in my room laying in my bed. My son just got out of school and I'm waiting for him to come home. He likes to walk home from school. In back of my bed is a window. I'm laying down waiting for my son to come home. I looked up at the window and out my window is the front of my house. I listened to hear if my son is at the front door. The door is behind me. God said, "Did I make a mistake?"

I'm facing the window and the door to the front is behind me, being the front of the house too.

If I face the front door, the window is behind me. Where's the backyard?

I was driving home from work. I stopped in front of my house and looked at the front of the house. I see my window. I pictured myself looking out the window and the front door is behind me. I looked at the front of my house and I looked towards the backyard. I can see the backyard—and it's behind too.

(Revelation 21:16–20)

The city was laid out like a square, as long as it was wide. He measured the city with the rod and found it to be 12,000 stadia in length, and as wide and high as it is long. The angel measured the wall using human measurement, and it was 144 cubits thick. The wall was made of jasper, and the city of pure gold, as pure as glass. The foundations of the city walls were decorated with every kind of precious stone. The first foundation was jasper, the second sapphire, the third agate, the fourth emerald, the fifth onyx, the sixth ruby, the seventh chrysolite, the eighth beryl, the ninth topaz, the tenth turquoise, the eleventh jacinth, and the twelfth amethyst.

I can be taken out anytime.